unrest
in the
nebulae

WRITING MATTERS!

A SERIES EDITED BY ALEXIS PAULINE GUMBS, MONICA HUERTA, ERICA RAND, AND JERRY ZEE

unrest in the nebulae

gitan djeli

Duke University Press
Durham and London 2026

© 2026 DUKE UNIVERSITY PRESS
All rights reserved
Project Editor: Bird Williams
Designed by Dave Rainey
Typeset in Untitled Serif and Malaga by Copperline
Book Services

Library of Congress Cataloging-in-Publication Data
Names: Djeli, Gitan, [date] author
Title: unrest in the nebulae / Gitan Djeli.
Other titles: Writing matters! (Duke University Press)
Description: Durham : Duke University Press, 2026. |
Series: Writing matters!
Identifiers: LCCN 2025028060 (print)
LCCN 2025028061 (ebook)
ISBN 9781478038504 paperback
ISBN 9781478033608 hardcover
ISBN 9781478062103 ebook
Subjects: LCSH: Imperialism—Poetry | Slavery in literature—
Poetry | LCGFT: Poetry | Prose poems
Classification: LCC PR9408.M273 D54 2026 (print) |
LCC PR9408.M273 (ebook) | DDC 821/.914—dc23/eng
/20251208
LC record available at https://lccn.loc.gov/2025028060
LC ebook record available at https://lccn.loc.gov/2025028061

Cover art and interior illustrations: Dipa Mahbuba Yasmin

contents

shaping ground together

gratitude to writers and poets who craft
oceanspheres of understanding one can rest in
and absorb the magnitude

i hope the lines reach you like they arrived
in waves in urgency in moments of clarity in
times when everything collapses

this murmuration of poems was written through
the lens of an oceanic historymaking and a
visualsonic archive of the kreol oceanlands in
Ziwa Kuu the deep waters—disnamed indian
ocean by coloniser-enslavers

unrest in the nebulae slow reads the everyday
geography of history—marked by *post-1492*
extractive logics of colonisation it draws from
anticolonial writings Black study queer loving
and from

*stories in tongues of ancestors from lands continents stories that do not
discover voyage arrive and settle*

the book of poetic utterances as method
experiments with the materiality of an
atmospheric worldmaking plausible living
through the wounds of this human epoch it halts
genocidal narratives of exploration conquering
possession ownership and weaves in a cosmo-
geological historiography

it attempts to disrupt the vocabulary and
grammar of war and economy that characterise
narratives of nationalist history writing

the nebulae situate five hundred years of unrest
exploitative colonisation ecocide extinction
militarisation and deportation slavery indenture
negotiated nationhood postcolonial plantation
structures and apologist histories

a collection in conversation with a lineage of
Caribbean poetics and philosophy from Kamau
Brathwaite to Sylvia Wynter it underlines the
afterlives of slavery with postindependence
prison institutions from another sea it unrests
with languaging as a possible process of
performing the future of abolition on the page

the nebulae also radiate a certain opacity and
tenderness of voice to create space for repair—
tending to our frequency restoring broken
histories holding safe moments from
generational hurt geographies of harm
surveillance profiling and policing structures of
distress

it is guided by and guides towards the sonic
resonance of a reciprocal rhythm a kreol call-and-
response poetics and sea shanties to situate rituals
flows occurrences and practices

most tenderly it is a wave of prose poems about
tongues and songs and conversations on
archipelagoes of lands and peaks that witness life
and living through the catastrophe of our times

~

apr. six pelabuhan ratu

spirit queens of southern seas
nyai rårå kidul manimekhala dewi kadita

for millennia moved earth with their waters
feathers waterborne seeds
ferns moss spores
whole trees wind drifted birds and bats
and sepals out of the whorl
fluttered sprinkled gathered

by the currents

~

lands of the unwinged biped

rårå

fluid h.er arms lace in a dance above their crown
of hair before shadows collide she floats on and in
the seas

underwater their world the skies her cosmos sh.e
watches over how light strikes between and within
clouds sometimes from fog to ground

shores horizons her being one with the surface
neck immersed their legs sleek fins iel slides
against liquid lava from

the rub the distance the depth the fissures the
groans and growls as air expands lungs
compresses a hundred times normal atmospheric
pressure

she arises from the valley her lips taste of seafoam
stars

iel.and

specks of land craters grumbled from ocean floors
eight million years igneous rocks ancient polyps red
mangroves

mantle home to grounddwelling giants sea cows keel-
scaled boas wedgetailed shearwaters parakeets

isle/land named renamed unnamed man-named dotted
by maps

archipelago   of   lands

flattened framed from settler orientation extraction
subtraction where life ogled of its last breath from a
fraction of a grid topography

the blue mountains have witnessed they remember
they murmur the story of geography

wrapped in a cloud

sipping tea at six in the morning is like being wrapped in a cloud she tells
me s'envelopper dans un nuage outside the world is a fog hazy sombre
unsettling unfluffy one that does not snuggle it moves across atmosphere
lays low slithers on asphalt muddles side grass on sharp edges pavements
borders grid-like roads swirls round knotty trunks oak trees cuts through
bones and flesh and lingers in sinus uninvited a misty one although there
is more visibility in mist the cloud she tells me does not numb nor hold
moisture from nearby bodies of water moist grounds marshes waterways
green algae formation on surfaces opaque rivers the cloud that nuzzles hair
and nestles in between breasts moves from ocean cumulus ancestors read
as unstormy weather and warm skies and sea whispers and tattooed arms

mountains on seas

deep breath slow push pulse of tissue shred of crystals a
quake from the core
crack of tectonic plates
the wake of kumarikkantam

lava spasms walls contract from the cosmic lining
of an orb a tremor first gasp oxygen release

a promise decibels mount cacophony
earthing from screams

and then silence fallen stars

liquid solidifying into blue basalt

usulu: planet in emakhuwa

she asks to imagine stories in tongues of ancestors from
lands continents stories that do not discover voyage arrive
and settle

sea currents flow ripple wind shift as planets rotate and
radiate the ocean gyre and swirl from indonesian
archipelagoes to the african sea and brush against cliffs of
the kreol isles spiral around madagaskan coral reefs and
sweep shoals of mozambik the spirits do the same they
continue to gather roam and guide   an ancient story
circulates

on the shores of moma that seapeople across times have
followed the movements of the great salty lake and
travelled to the islands twelve families sustained by the
ocean today retell how lost at sea currents returned them
to the continent to the same coastline where captured
emakhuwa ancestors rebelled on ships sang and danced
tufu from which they composed sega

for nations people have followed rhymes of planets and
moons and tides and sea currents and ocean lands

cosmic blue february twenty-nine

her glitter hair a smooth waterfall shaved on the side a
playful wisp by her ear a smile the size of that last
weekend in covent garden a portal between the before
and the after

a dream night she writes as it closes and opens to

timeclouds marked by watching two silhouette ravens
for hours from her window a couple they perch on the
highest evergreen conifer its tip weeping in a curve
she snaps movement of them flying away one after
the other against silver pastel warm and maroon skies

down below the scattered coo of a northern
hemisphere wood pigeon as it lands on the shed picks
from a bird feeder round confident haughty it flaps its
body to the lawn observes left right on the side eyes
and head roll three toed foot firmly on ground it
waddles around undisturbed unaffected

it knows the land a long time a habitat vascular forest
thirst rivers silence mists homo economicus turned
into landscape and property and named itself a species
above all lives

ground.

pause

read once

stay on one word
one line one stanza one page stay
for an hour a week a month a year or more

the nebulae begin as a genealogy of geography of an
unwinged biped its spirit on the land from an ocean current and sky
navigation from people travelled across land masses and geological times
from archipelagos of land named from tongues imagined

and birds mapped the skies as vibration life forms
as particles think with the lands the seasons

build your khashaba
pause pause a lot

makook eit

whroo whroo throaty lengthened grunt in sönényö nicobarese
the bipeds bond is the makook from the battimalv isle eit to
which they fly back before the swirl of the southwest
monsoon where they roost

kalos beautiful oinas dove from an ancient greek language
pale natural scientists fixated on to identify classify
categorise a genus a taxonomic rank below in order to
document compile

archive hierarchise the odd the fanciful the different the
familiar bird the biologically bias prescription phylogeny
silencing the repetitive ancestral whoooo of muluku

the closest living relative is a bright feathered goura mostly
grounddwelling who arrive on chowra island with the rains
after peak summer

tītī

a long gone caloenas speckled green and white *tītīhope'ore*
recalled from tahiti as the shadow of the mountain gods they
flew from the pacific to the southern seas

its other cousins two bipeds of the kreol isles their names
runaway captives gave in fon emakhuwa wolof tamil
malagasy bambara bangali are long lost with their tongues
and tales

playful noisy carefree the ground their sky on which they
walked free stunned to become prey to capital unaware of
hunted northern birds and homo erectus

they join the bedrocks from where they flew

the captive boy and the unwinged biped

we still colour the skies of the nicobar isles and follow the currents sea
and winds one storm thousand years ago we swirl loop low

for nights wings broken we collapse on warm basalt hearts pumping
under iridescent blazing ocean scapulars upper neck

plumage wrenched in salt water metallic green copper hackles dead short
and white tail twisted i lift my small blackish beak my strong legs

and feet dull and bleeding bright my irides dark my vision flutter
monocular blurred sunlight i breathe many cannot a few of us

survive we grow walking aves for millennia seeing colour bipeds like us
come and go until we hear for the first time from ships

mauritshuis amsterdam hollandia duyfken pale hunters of trees of sky of
ancient visitors of us we remember a sun kissed boy break free from

the hold takes refuge deep inland he runs until wind stops to whistle he
knows he reaches dense woods at tranquil rivering streams

bwapom leaves fandia ferns crunch he slows down listens our shrieks on
ground in branches on dark wood in air on water in exile

unfree fugitive he grows strong and tall and speaks in tongues and tones
away from those who poison land

his mothers name was not simon ours was not dodaar

kasuari/casuarina

filao kouma nou inn apel sa pie la koumsa it starts
with seducing her into a vortex of semantics how are
trees named not for taxonomy phylogeny the
subtraction of botany and taxidermy

filao difil lao hanging string fibre strand thread cord
filament casuarina at least dropped from the
indonesian kasuari on the aru islands the iri-an lands
this majestic two-metre tall matriarch of a bird a kasu
on its head leathery black string fil filament get lao

lapis lazuli neck blue of an outer world the same
power legs long three-toes feet sharp claws that
ministered the final blow

the same ferocity soliter from the isle of the east on
arab maps gone the same way from a seventeenth-
century travelogue

. . . when irritated they whirled about twenty or
thirty times on the same side for four or five minutes,
rattling their wings and making a noise like thunder
that could be heard an eighth of a mile away

her first question was *Simon* from the malay world
names of captives silenced rebels from muluku
batavia haunt the archives of the kreol isles my
resonant wonder was how the only trace that shapes
symbiosis not from imposed relations and
contemptuous residues

gets dismissed over and over as fantasy

lexotik

the ones planted at home are crowded spiky frisky
orange and bluish birdflowers grow in disarranged tall
leafy bushes homes of flies spiders mould they are
river foliages that scratch bite itch into dust

two nude stems of a burung cenderawasih in fabric an
intricate arrangement perched on a stem a prolonged
pike on an inverted flamingo leg a groundless
apartment an ornament

rendered exotic refined to lifeless unnatured splitting
monstrous leaves killing the abundance of mess and
decay making it politely lovely

accessories she says and kindly rolls her eyes

nautical twilight

we witness at a transition of atmosphere in the centre of east
and west a bed of mountains and moss sitting on the same sea
three hundred years later starting to buzz

one spot one section of the canopy on the circular line of the
green horizon a lowland cluster on a specific dot from our view
point a forest on the ocean wake up and murmur and reach us
across sea lake to the tip of the bay we slept on

. . . there are birds that shriek like humans, they are in holes
under the earth and if one had not found them, one would have
said that it was a rabble, as they shriek all night long especially
in the morning, because there were sailors that went towards
the shrieking and took the birds out of the holes

another extractive travelogue

that birds are tuned to three dawns every morning in astronomy
referred to civil   six degrees below the skyline
nautical   twelve degrees and   astronomical twilight
eighteen degrees

the concentus behind dawn chorus how when and why they
roost when thousands of birds gather in a tree patch at sunset
and wake through three dawns and fly out at the third sign of
light

how they shriek at threat how they keep land awake we stand
still and listen and watch the still waters mirror their morning
flight

hide manumèʻa hide

from nuʻulua on savaiʻi the unwinged biped hears you long high
pitch whistly oooh the same órnīs family flowing from the
currents of the continuous oceanic flow

we shared the same respiratory particle

until that flight across the only explanation a magnetic shift from
cosmic storms every thousand human years and a break in
molecular existence defined not by millennia but the
astrophysical event the racial event the extractive rebellion event

the possibility of avian plasma or the gill arches in our throat at
four weeks in the womb for ocean breathing is in the enclosure
of salt sugar and the cosmos

pijin

ouwhrōō oõ-óû-oo õuw-hū õuw-hu low krooling throaty pitched repetitive calls our pijin djinn once used to guide birds from one island to the other

pidjins have twenty-seven to fifty-nine taste buds if or when their beaks hurt from damage their tongues wither and die the grounddwelling kasuari ostrich emu rhea and kiwi have small triangular tongues that do not reach the tip of their

bill they screech they call they sing they dream they mutter they croak they creak they squeak they roar they swallow small stones to grind up seeds moored of tambalakok and insects

brown bipeds finding refuge on cliffs and coastal reefs their feet in light stellar an ave exposed by torn ebony this is how an island becomes a continent to be pillaged

tongues ruffle flap they once gave the forests its sound a pidgin is a tongue and a sonic geography

mo zwazo rouz

the wake the clamour olive red necked fodies
cuckooshrike cardinals weave shriek hiss grey martin myna sparrows
pick peck poke bulbul pink

pigeon striped herons night oggle gobble oukoul an
orchestra from one specific spot on the mountains pull open our
wooden door our sleep still

breathing dreamscapes a wake a geography that calls
speaks cries that sentence i remember imagine land as soundscape sky
as loud trees

thumping life of songbirds and feathers and flaps and
tongues

a cacophony in history we promise to return to

membered.

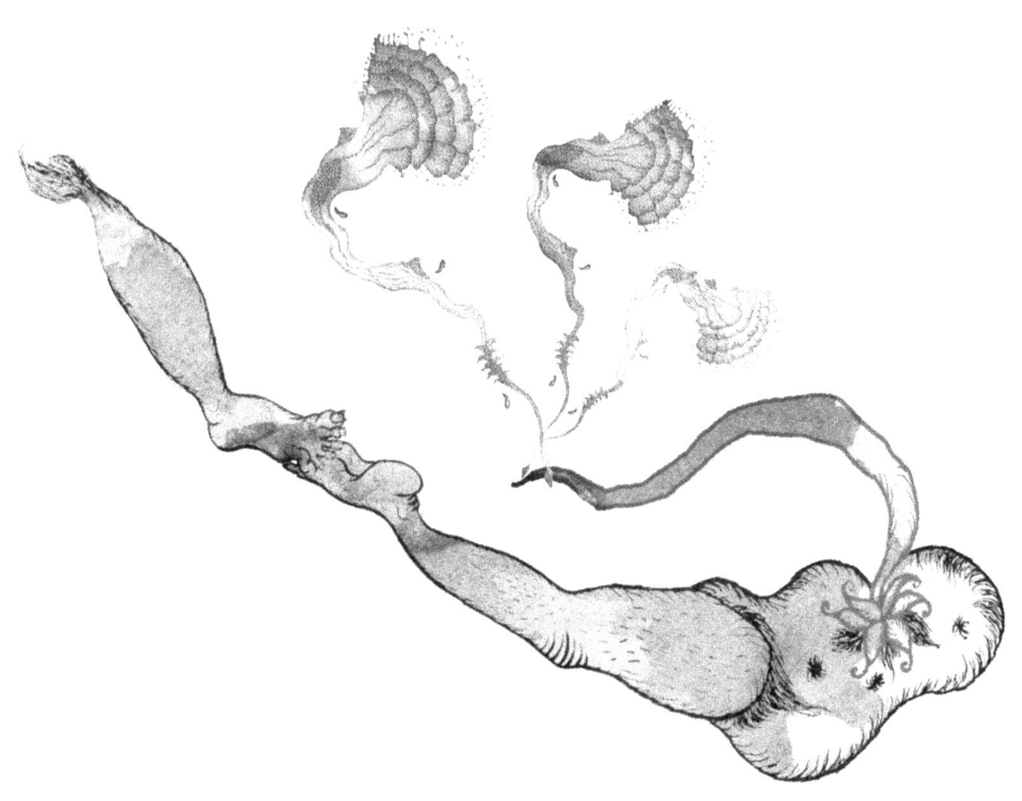

stay

on the metaphor stay on
the imagery the associated thought
stay until it requires distance and discomfort

start again sit in fiction
slow read other genres read ancestral
thinkers think with them think with the skies the seasons
pause pause a lot then read again with presence

with knowing scroll read listen watch
understand five hundred years of racial disaster capitalism
unrest in the nebulae is homed in this lineage
in storytelling that refuses

read between alphabets words lines
viewpoints contextualise organise unfamiliar bibliographies
ungendered grammars read the omission
the unsaid

~

homo narrans

nihiko ni nimozhá, kahkumaka kanrohaka
elapó eh mozha kahaka eleliwa sana

once upon a time i travelled to a place
where i was well received
—storytelling opening in emakhuwa

~

language as spirit-tongue

story of words in sound

ravenala lapis lazuli seeds three hundred years her
hair ran down in red braided rivulets from a history of
words in sound in patterned wrappers silver bangles
copper anklets head beads clay faces

the tsimihety never trim their hair and do not bow to
merina monarchs

betrayed by kings and coastal kins she reaches the
batavia shores and descends to pulicat from
betsimisaraka retrieved from the legal ledgers of
resistance and violence and the silences in the archive
esperance was baptised on a slave ship

esperance *named* hope *for who*   on this soil

kreol li son avan langaz non

she blurts out stormy thoughts about tongue being sound first
before becoming language and music silence is sound her gateh
her rotten her love muses over the music in mayot and komor
how they had something of sega but not quite the emakhuwa
tufu in the inland mountains of mozambik her uncle felt the
island pulse in his veins

the kreol tongue was sound first before language and music she
stays on this is music not sound and language she voices out
loud how the kreol isles moris sesel reinyon shagos rodrig
agalega their sega moutia maloya makalapo tanbour sega ariko
kadriy akordeon sharing beats and rhythms and history of
enslavement   this is language

how sound and words come to existence we ponder our eyes
thinking through a sonic frequency women children men
captured separated across islands how they conceived language
from sound uttered how they spoke among themselves from the
pain the terror the dream of otherwise where how when was it
bellowed how it became language of a nasyon

from the inlands or on the east shores ports from the sea
sickness of the hold on the decks on other lands in plantation
rooms in the fields when how while labouring new soils
planting sugar cutting sugar fining sugar breaking stones
breastfeeding pale mouths   while at dusk in the lucid
dreaming of their ocean floors

a rhythm that rises as they tinkle a metal spoon rattle seeds in
bamboo shoots shake sand in tins clap tap feet whistle hoot
choul made instruments from goat skin worked stretched
smoothed from soft wood bent circled tied from kalbas
squashed hollowed bellowed from tired hands flat drummed
into floods and storms

unrest one

june thirty

a.dark silhouette in an in.dis.tin.ct sky patch. bright. settling dust from the cornea of a.blurred vision

a.blue dressing gown i stare at a three quarter wax.ing.moon waiting for a boat june 1695 ana and esperance of bangal rises to the settlement to sugar poison to the rats their swarm their arms bamboes antoni from coromandel and anbon aaron from muluku paul from batavia

a.map they drew of the house they smelled the wind the direction the covered spaces the trees the bushes captured the exit times the creaking noises made love broke the locks

a.lodge they burned the enslavers den raised the cotton curtains flaming towards the tangerine trees bougainvillea and lemongrass fixed to the cross their liberation dreams hopes

a.haunting on the land seeped in their wounding in which we walk ruins that shatter the sphere our bodies carrying the shiver and the unrest

a.history in unfreedom   from the house of unreparative justice

rise of tongue

knots press on airways
burst thyroid gland
hear the silence
refrain.
a voice rises from lime sea
foam

feet stomped under ochre suns
rains chains escapes
tied to exist
rest.
a smack of life betrays the
womb

moon fucks sun at dawn
blights misty ebony trees
grounded in hope
resist.
a prelude to blue-tongued
mornings

skin scars into river keloids
ancestral tongues moan
itches and twitch
rebirth.
a lalang kreol sputter in calico
red

ocean skies washes soothes
holds the land rustles in tears
a call to recall
rhyme.
a ritual rises in stories and
songs

arbre:pye

i wonder how tree
became foot in kreol i
wonder how tree became
at the foot in kreol i
wonder how tree became
au pied de l'arbre in kreol
how tree became au pied
du mur in kreol became
coup de pied sous l'arbre

a european genealogy of
kreol tongues unsilencing
colonial archives
sounding captives from a
plantation that uprooted
to plant itself how pye
sprung from wolof fon
malagasy emakhuwa i
can only hope evoke

that trees ont aussi les pye
sur terre but they walk
trees ont un pye quelque
part and their roots move
trees play frôlent le pye
de quelqu'un play brush
against trees also stand
pye à pye retombent sur
ses pye reprennent sur un

bon pye vivent sur un
grand pye trees also
listen and tell stories
improvised under trees music
composed under trees joy danced
under trees care
happened under
trees

tongues grow under trees

six eight

iel sits slender a wave she holds that drum
an extra organ in the evening smoke of
her cousins place

six eight six eight six eight six eight

slow it starts
slow it waves slow it beats
slow it moves up tongues hips feet

it sizzles songs speech sound
it stomps earth in gold and orange hues

and then it rises sega
in tempo in rhythm
in beats and dance
it builds it plays it shakes walls and towers
it mixes soil and sky it merges blood
and sweat
it fuses oceans and continents

in kreoling creating creare to create
to make as it goes k not c
kreoling autopoiesis self creating

world making

lalang twist

my tongue mutters a p at p at wa
a poetry of brevity in acoustic effect
it rolls clinks spits without caesural comma
pours from the pit of my affective stomach

ayo do baba
my francofied té lé g ou rhymes an island breeze
a song mixed in bo hoj poo ri chautals
it coils loops twists with a street syntax
flows from the pot of a sanskritised creole

atchia bheti
my grandmother calls from goodlands
a sonic rhapsody of the senses
she scolds reeks shrieks with no full stop
ghosts from the still of my memory bank

ale vini a n ou ale
my lips repeats two sonic negations
e k ou te vi ni vi ni hear hear come come I say
it booms roars looms with its own grammar
marks from the archives of a silenced history

lalang twist
my body dances to metric syllables
deranging the parataxis archive
it stirs links kicks with no syntactic connector
blows from the mind of visc e ra li ty

my voice flutters within four tongues
a transit of worlds in one world
it chinks ticks clicks in bass and high frequencies
songs from the chime of a muted sonata

sonic.

creation sounds

she reads that the words wilderness and control do not surface
in land languages that do not extract that creation worlds were
wavelengths vibrations and frequencies

that silences in the isles forests cannot hold form of overtone
whistles of the wind throats of deep wood high nasal pitch
birdcalls deafening timbre of caves

that origin stories of the last five hundred years or two
thousand years or fourteen billion years are fractured the
beginning the linear white time causality

note the apterous resonance of twigs of capsules of seawater of
under riverskies of follicles magnified to saltitude note the
drum of ocean gathering and friction against croak and silt note
life from dust from the troposphere

next door the akordeon mavarann plays against the coming
storm

ore oru oorile

two hundred years ago in that place three
messengers floated on the docks until they
lock spirits in the soil a kalimaye grew from
the   earth and lores of two continents and
three oceans seeded

to suck the sugar poison sisters placed seven
stones under a banyan tree for there were no
neem they spread cockerel blood sindoor
candles and lamps to rally women and revel
in the colours of tree root storytelling and
evening baithkās

to teach in kreol tamoul bojpouri old tongues
and new tongues from ancestral lines

unrest two

seventeen march

i.woke up scared 2:13

i.write not feeling good. was supposed to be at airport at six was with a lover in a bathrobe after having sex in that house. i did not need to go after all i was not comfortable people debating somebody made a joke to climb the queen window the sister was cooking a dish of dhal

i.write a gun to my head worried of dying waken from a dream of dust and gatherings 1943 soondrun pavattan with sticks and stones and bare arms rises to the plantation to ashy chimneys to the brutes

i.am silenced nationalism monumentalises her unhistoricises the shooting the police the men who pointed guns to the workers

never held to account

the unspirited

why churayil stay with us

to yama lok we perform *deep daan* to bring relief to
their roaming the eldest in the household faces southern
oceans and a lamp lit   nobody looks at the
flame

and if a churayil cries out in the night we sit in silence
for her to leave the inbetween after evoking three times
the dead in us the plantation holds too many mother and
child churayil across fields across lands

too many undead she replies

unrest three

saturday nineteen

i.dream of one orca and a doormat and i am bored. i seal my sharks in bubble wrap envelopes. when i take them out the orca holds my ankle and explodes. seems i left the front door open and the gate. strange feeling nauseous morbid that i am being observed

i.go down a hotel lobby to tell them. they send a container to save us not a boat. they say we speak of ungratitude. they disapprove. it is shabby the hotel blue in the shape of a pyramid like the sept cascades building in port louis but faded with black lines of mould

i.wont go in. i end up in the back busy roads of a dusty city. i walk around unfamiliar settings. sweaty evening people sing and mourn. i am relieved i escape the container was cut in half and covered with fabric

i.do not poetise 1968 lisette talate with seawater and two thousands of her kins tend to displacement to governments to geopolitics the status of women committee does not cover the rights of birds they live

i.read the police threatened her with rape lose her children to keep her in perpetual unfreedom the law conceived on stolen land

coralground

for you manjula varshni and oli gianni and darius

her school had spirit stayed open and relished in new waves and sounds
and worlds hummed from the overstated set of stairs

her voice pierced across institutional doors punctured by scents of
chickpeas samousas and chapatis she always broke them in two

pieces of lalo dab of bred sonz binds molecules to ancestry immune from
patriarchy next door in a fragile beard and three pairs of eyes

strength of her base her presence transfused in cells and chords and
charcoal the drumming of pains and sweats

and shared musks and aromas of bounded affinity magnetised haloed in
the attraction of unlike polar shifts

she drove bare feet the pressure of a survivor she knew it they knew it
hurt from the vengeance of a trust

until the height of the fall the moment of splitting and inevitability
when her chest ripped apart

she wanted to believe in the improbability that she would not break the
phenomena of life here not when them two were still singing

songs that erase shadows build towers gave her life mourned past lives
celebrated amber futures lulled her present life

her stride stands as reminiscence as her two polyps spring firmly upward
across an indigo stretch of the lagoon

unrest four

twenty-first february

i.write a clouded reality

i.search through death certificates after 1999 vijay nancy yousouf mohamad muthy ganeshlall juggernath joseph reginald topize clency jacquotte afzal seekundar jay ramloll   dead by the national police

i.do not hear their fears as in 1943 the colonial edifices of punishment permitted to violate and unprotect and continue five hundred years of carceral violence

i.wake in sweats and chest in the shower the mother joins us pumping against my breasts 1 june 2020 marie rose randamy

i.watch the police evicts her during a pandemic for growing a garden on state wasted land to feed seven orphans she homed

i.hear her scream in pain the injustices of the prison island that privatises soil and seas under her ancestors feet in which she walks   until she breathes out bees to abolish the plantation

sonotopological shift

the land on the east coast where the ku dwell invites us
to their kaya dwelling sacred home for canopy

for inner woods with sound and flow land that words
within the contour of shores

the archipelago sits on ocean frequencies echoed from
the middle land the same kaya agathe fanfan menwar

from the seven earths soley rouz micheline marlène tidal
bloodlines of salt and spice and coloured soil and seeds

carried in the mesh of hair braided with bark sap resin
and kokiy portboner only vocal in translation

magmatic shifts with the cosmos that call for rituals of
sound where voice simmers into chords and drums

and forest silences and snail grounds

unread

always unread
colonial syllabi take years
of unreading unread institutional knowledge

the footnote is often the main text unthink
postindependence narratives unlearn linear progress unsee
colonial museums unthink creation stories science discipline
rethink new genealogies then find repair in the nebulae

rewire into collage the weather
reminder of settler colonialism from the Americas
to Gaza to every particle of toxin in the air and the waters
undo words with any trace of violence war power undo
vocabularies of exploitative economy

write notes in
your mothers tongue in your
grandmothers voice think in tongues your blood
carries in tongues you know abounds in the whispers
of rain think with the cosmos

how does it spark life

ice pick stars.

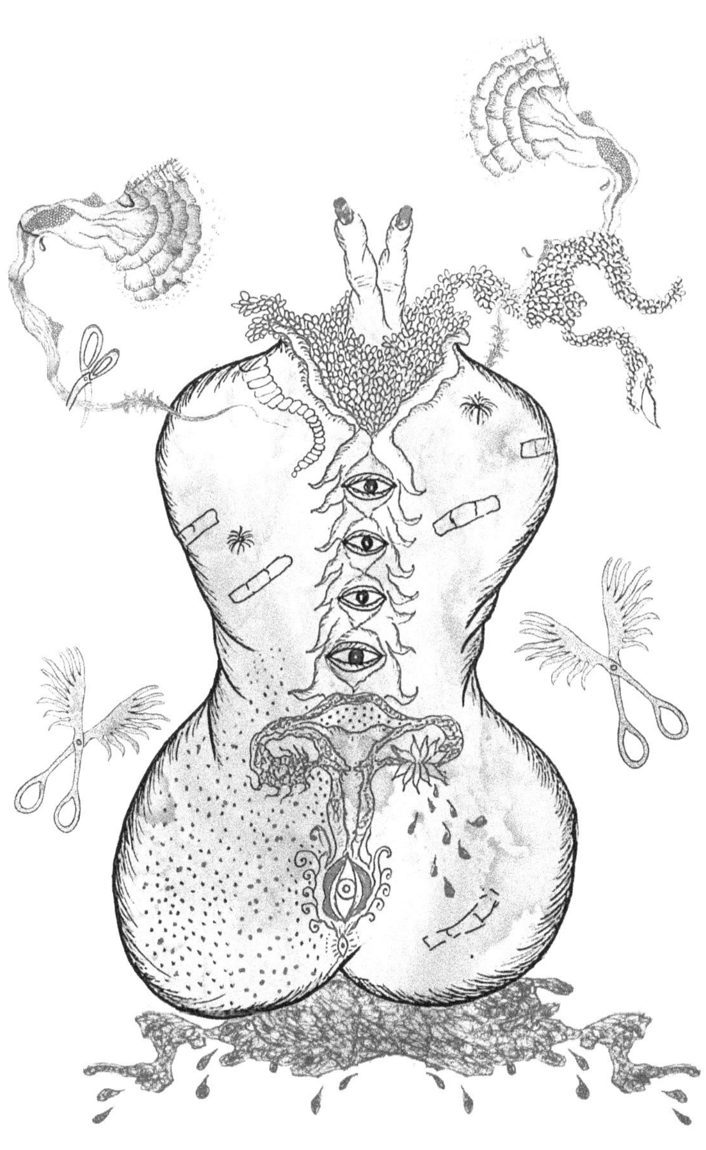

~

smothering island

i wimble across dons on mothers day
between sticks n sushi and odeon centre point and polka theatre

the whisper of her unfreedom brushes against my unrest

~

bone-deep lineage

cell nephology

at three months in her mothers waters the mother carried
her daughter in particles of dust seven million of them a
nebula

an ancestral cell in a vessel held by the lining the intrusion
that it could not expel an absorption of a lineage that
becomes the formation of the molecular now the present
moment of the here

to recompose inaudible life in vials of isopropyl and
translucent bodies is to repeat the harm the hurt the wound

repair is only the island tip on a mountain sea the swirl of
the ocean tends to bloodlines of watersky protectors

moonlines

horizontal the new norm in cosmological time the only
constance was the cyclical moon midst of night she
swiped and the rest became torrent

mornings were paler blended pastels shell-blush in the
west fading into grey-blues a noncolour of dust and
light northern skies uniform washed out on the island
horizon sea merge into spheres clothes hanging on a
windless day

the textuality of voice with sky as guide there was
something of that sea that movement that dip that
strength that gaze that search that intrigued troubled
gathered made their stomach throb that knowing that
presence that expanse of waterfall waterrocks deep
blues fluid an atmosphere above

so slender their molecular core hurt fingers that clicked
flicked flapped that explored landscape captured held
cupped mouthed that comforting stillness oceanic drop
she kept hold a raw flow they slept replied trickled a fall
a detailed precise route they held onto every curb every
bump every nook

a crevice they smoothed over and over

mitochondria of wounds

they read zami then still i rise and caged bird her heart races her pulse
whizzes her blood pressure mounts breathe deeply she says hold your
breath release slowly they say and walk out of the safe

bars break in scorched hands the seventy four year old mother waddles on
her feet in pain to be seen by the fed placed on a pedestal to raise her high
so she never rises from her smile at his birth   her sadness that
followed now eats the seeds of bitterness and grieves in cruelty

her nebula walks for hours across the canal round the grid in circular
eights to ease to release to shed the reunion of mother and bully of the
sister the cousin the wife who refuses to be caged refuses the block
painted with care where she is placed to slash her legs and let her bleed
until her womb splits

there are no free birds   by association an oxymoron

they then read ruby lips and wine tongues and pout and blink so she stops
thinking about cages and birds they calm the storm the flutter in her
stomach the bile that piles up in her throat the lump that grows on her left
shoulder the torment knifed in her back

they surface lips taste of grass and river water

the disorientation of punctuation

there are women who are apparitions their brokenness from
sons they monstered so deeply splintered in flesh that breath is
pulled out

arteries squeezed dry and eggshells puncture soles that harden
as they bleed there are women whose splinter grows so sharp
and acute that a

nightdress swallows them and drains kindness and tenderness

and then there are mothers their insides soured from bitterness
cruelty lost in a cycle of depthless pain they cannot rise from

a circle of hate and rage and despair a paralysis and the wounds
become palatable parasitical

a numb ache that stays a needle in a daughters breast

rapture

their breathing heavy loud exhaling fog upon chest every four seconds on a device on a pillow she wakes up in a mist storm of adjusting timezones moods weathers suns twilights the heat on their side central heat on hers reassured of connectedness their confusion eased unmuted with hearts writing iel in words like she reaches with voice a slow dance a low lying humid wrap under their feet on warm wood stones the whispers of her fingers pulling them to a slow point of constant return she writes herself on their skin in breath and morning slumber four thirty-two eight thirty-two volcanic silences when lava settles they make oceanlands of care *she hears them sleep and she drifts*

allodynia

she has this pain in her back under her left shoulder
blade that recurs she had this pain in her womb a hot rod
piercing her insides as she opens her eyes and reaches
out for brufen she has this shimmering pain on her
shoulders ice picks stars that burn her arms and then
sometimes she has the mattress scorch her skin dig a
hole and suck her flesh

the wounds that pin her down beg for pain from stimuli to
keep feeling she begs to be fucked hard until her
body container of pain releases storms and bees and
lakes and trickles to sleep

and then there is synaesthesia when they hurt and she
hurts and they know at the same time when they speak the
same word when she wakes her nightmare when she curses
pain before they write it down when she holds
their breathing to slow her heart when she tears down to
stay with them as they exhale decades of triggers and
open tears

she rises their lips taste of sweat and depth

karmic a long interval

the ballet dancer turns eighteen the year status and
independence ratified her options to wed or leave her
tongue she chose empire over patriarchy both nations
built on shifting the vibration of her stars

the one who broke the ballet dancer under a cold shower
called her haughtiness into disinheritance writes about
telegou hides under a borrowed tongue and cannot find
salvation in the tongues of those who still walk the soil
on our skin the dust we breathe

the house the ballet dancer is cast from the second
woman with thick curly hair sits under the same mango
tree we are asked to muster our clouds waiting to be
welcomed so the past can be pardoned and guilt can be
erased by charitable lies on a bed she returns to

the ballet dancer rides her grandfathers roadster bicycle
across sugar fields and swings from a banyan tree she
boards a train without a pram on a station she squanders
off when the city calls for the father to parent in voices
and musks they erase from their new grammar

the one who betrayed the ballet dancer studied while she
fretted from two blue lines carried from wimbledon on
roots routed in london to cranfield to luton during a heat
wave she carried in her waters

the ballet dancer birthed a daughter in two beds and
fields apart and wrapped her in scents of tongues
weaved to destinies carved by the logic of a rejected
union and a sister across the ocean in oblivion

the daughter wonders why her birth certificate is not in
her tongue spread vertical in red ink the word bedford
stands out a bedlock she splits from weekend nights

between gladstone and hill road her birth was a hurt she
forgave because it was life from a dying star

the one who left sellotaped top of the pops calendar on a
brown washed wall in a cramped apartment with
innocence seeped in guilt and harboured in silt clouded
nine months of unwombed life from three women who
weaved him out of their lores

the daughter searched the land with a grieved kiss of
delusional mournings an autumn walk with stardust of
expectation and shadows of karma his charm finding
solutions in isolation he finds her and parks at heathrow
his unfiled fine an unrest she carried for far too long

the ballet dancer returns to the nebula a bedford lorry
with cheeks and lashes three lines grinding a smile a
domed crest of harvested canes picked up the residues
and crowning despair and struggles to find a bedrock
she can afford in paradise

the daughter stole an old insect infested thin blue book
with her name in gold dust on the cover before that
room was fumigated and the house sold who it belonged
still intrigues her she retrieved and revealed her name
when theft and debt made sense

the father left the daughter among glass bottles and stars
on her thumb before she found out she was a poem
thirty years later he gifts her a bureau amidst crunched
perfumed papers with letterhead and healed wounds and
bonded tears

the daughter burns the note with dragon blood incense
when tongues songs voices and rhythms and life instill
the silenced punctuation of language she leaves on a
storm the only comfort the conversation in their eyes
and the roar in her crash helmet

curved horizon

our mother taught us how to back glide
open leg   centre the core   ground to/with the ocean
trust   you will not sink navel upward   thigh above water
skin reach sky   spread your arms   close your eyes

let your hair soak   root submerge   ear deep in water
soundplay against skin   fissle of the depth   flutter back
flat with the ocean   flat with the curved air   flat with the horizon
sea star   a confused gravity   and the body floats unfettered

as far from the shore it lays knowing
the drift leads to the   reefs   let go
cold dark slide in/under   from the abyssal zone
absorbed   between weight of sky   and depth of sea

a rhythm of unsinking

djinn

our aunts not only tell us to learn lesson and survive and be
marked by and beyond temporality when adrenaline pumps
and your heart throbs and limbs shake and pulse mounts in
hair that rivers to the surface conjuring the moons you
know what they mean to be marked by the history of a
place where a realm exists between land and water

they teach us to confide care and unhaunt they tell us on
such nights to release dreamare apparitions we remember
and retell them before midday to someone we love

the act of conjuring together form a ritual of salt and spit to
face and change images and spirits into speech and words is
to speak with and away sh.e sees her leave the room they
look around she moves the device

and here it is la dame blanche on the polystyrene cornice in
the ceiling of the room who shifts to the camera her eye the
size of a cambium lens on which her finger turns the screen
flesh orange they hear her nine thousand

kilometres away she screams of her aunt who they incensed
the previous day with opium sticks dried petals and
ancestral blood the aunt like the mother whose curse to the
lover who killed her they know is irretrievable

they emerge from southern lips and seas

blade.

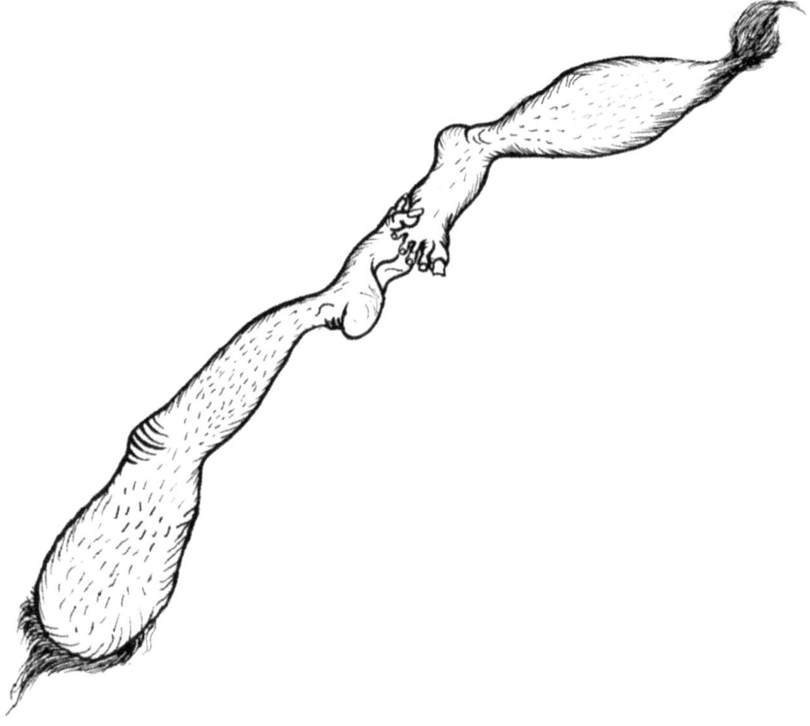

of drips and saltskies

they meet again on different shores tempers that storm
that blister she tells them of coffee and sugar routes
montanyar the upland roots sh.e hears screened relations
stalagmites on opiate narratives of preach

there are stories of origins of water drips into columns
soil into rivers in the depth of land between ocean
sediments and calcified histories

on the isle of fifty two curves they land on the shoal
ocean ridge where the other alchemist fills up shelves at
our arrival the only yellow metals are blazed skies
unthreatened streets unheard on the mainland

she speaks of floods sh.e hears ceilings of salt so they
walk out of the hollow night a cavernous promise they
needed to break

unsafe sands

she calls the mother on her seventieth three years
since she spoke to her she holds iels hand one screen
behind who recalls the girl who likes rulers and she
stumbles in fleshy smiles

tikopin the mother surprises them she feels the two
valves of her heart pump cells one pulls in one
blows out she sees a pulse reading poor on a blood
pressure monitor her hearts eyes sprung out of her
socket her long fingers on her forehead unprepared
holding her chest as it constricts and expands the
hurt physically prompting her to flee prompting her
tongue to utter in distress in honesty

tikopinn she waits the mother stares at her she
struggles not to disappear the space charged
slighting kilometres of ocean lands and thinning
oxygen in between two hemispheres she stays to
believe to wait for relief

when the mother says well if its love . . . *they lock*
eyes and pressure subsides into ripples of sand

punctured stars

they read the weather from the colour shape dispersion scattering
sound of clouds the moon rising from northern isles where freedom
thinkers were exiled and setting on lion mountain the view triggering
flight from enslavers ships eight fugitives would live inland and never
return to the continent

they watch a thick line of dark blue in between sky and canopies and
mountains a thick dash between and above bodies of leaves that thin
line under the atmosphere gaseous expansion she did not want to see
the ocean on her flight as they approach land

there is something with nacreous topviews that flashes of unfluid
bounded and bordered postcards that pulls her to a vertiginous fall
many sit and rest in the sight and wait and breathe the scape

they immerse themselves in the proximity of the ocean crowning their
cheeks and forehead she lies and her mother surfaces   in her red
mini with stars punctured in its floor driving to the sea bare feet a
glow on her dark freckled face pareo around her thin neck a glee as
she brakes

leaves us and hurries to ground her feet in wet sands before we three
straddle along she picked a handful of fat grains basalt stones shiny
grey specks translucent shells brown pastel corals history and
geography yesterday they rest in her palm as water seeped through
weight amplified by lightness

~

unmake

when words and voice lick you river deep and liberate

and you dance up to diamonds on repeat and gasp for air
as egos and nations break

~

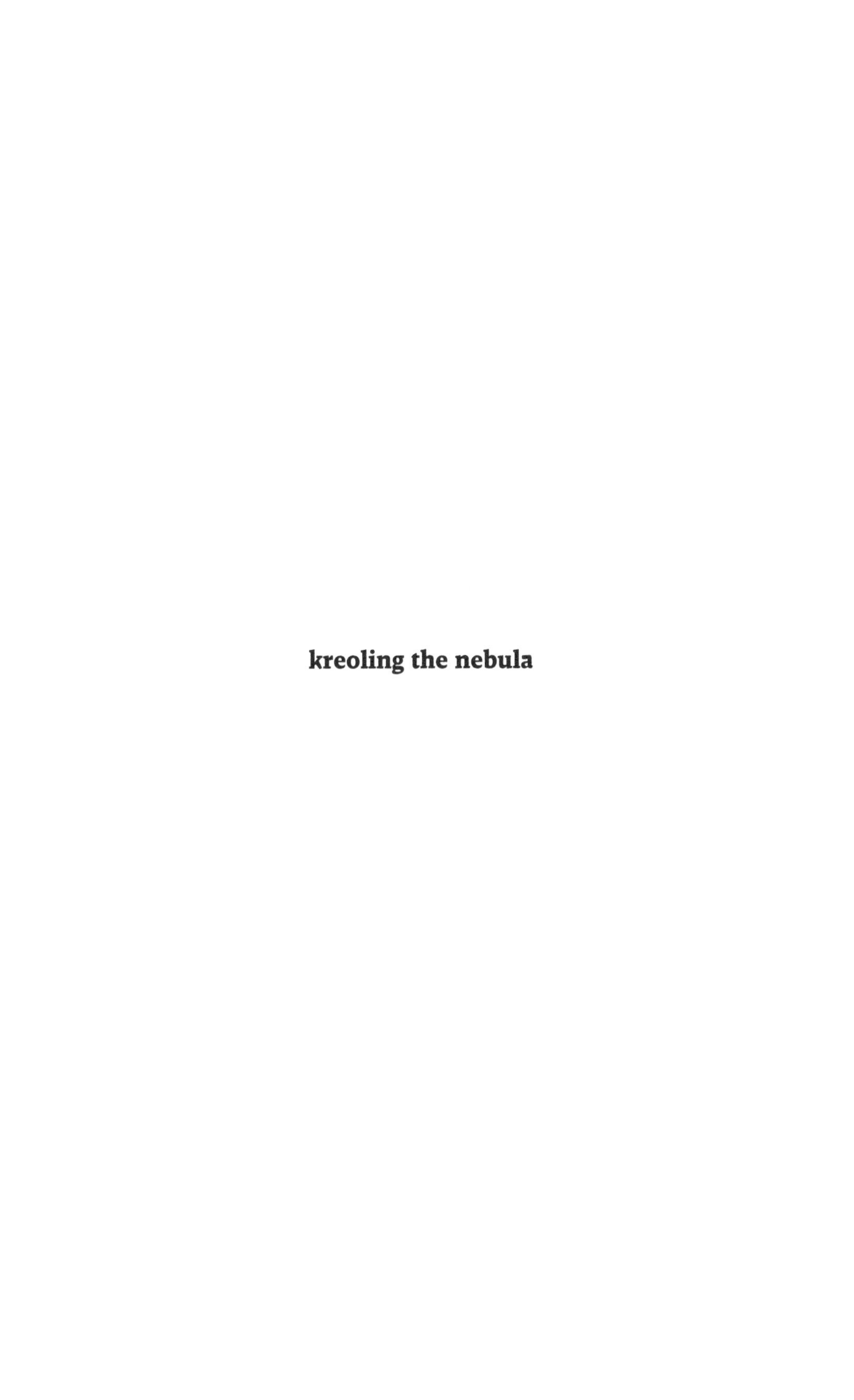

kreoling the nebula

restart

disrupt
the passive voice question
the i the we who is we find comfort
in protest question the arithmetics of violence

think with abolition as toolbox framework guideline
to abolish plantation cartographies state genocides
carceral punishment systems of law

then restart synchronise the unrest with that
genealogy create punctuations of methodological
tenderness from an atmosphere of loving presence
from an otherwise timeline

a new cosmogony reread rephrase
restore rest in the nebulae how do we imagine
from the ashes and organise from the page

riri

free floating she walks the red velvet in shimmer unsettles
colonial post nations her spire points to the skies across
fabric above a birdcrown maze plaited in lace
unapologising from honorary to ambassador of the isles

isle.land to the core

queendom a trinity of celestials aspires a kreol nation in
being in becoming in the making

in beads in peacock wings and feathers in make.up in criss
cross tights and heels in diplomacy in emerald blues in
smiles that conch shell a people in pride

as crop over takes place expands sugar to the bedazzled
rhinestone chalice in tattooed ringed nailed hands and
ensembles

she stars the cosmos a generation at her light

vertigo

the horizontal is always curved to the magnetic core
the reflexologist read it in the contours of her flat
soles

she imagines repair mending tending to what she
endures standing from the extractive logic of
everyday white conscience

over the south atlantic the field signals a frequency
coincidently from the repository of five centuries of
excess salt in the ocean enclosure

she is advised to rest and align to wounded waters in
her ear orchestral flutter of birds disoriented by callus
blood and oceansphere

and a high pitch vibration in her head

skylore

krios moon: courage to oneself she reads

she whispers that the elders taught them to
harvest the fatak grass on moonless nights when
it flowers and separates into hundreds of fine
fronds to delay the decay of finished brooms

unripe it leaves tiger stars under their feet

locating spica: reassess enter and maintain
unions from a place of honesty seek
commitment to sail seas that shore your flows
in a place of trust pause and recalibrate

the lores were written in the winds

she whispers it all started with a blood moon
on a night where twirled tongues pearls of
sweat and wordy ropes grounded the earth and
opened the universe under her feet

they continue to read in the silence of new
cosmogonies

rivers of words

she hulahoops days of holding the circle to hold her
if being held was not the reason holding to movement
was she dances six times a week like life depends on
it through tears and trepidation she feels her arm
resist a lead bar unwilling to engage

she holds persist muscle burns chills cold sweats she
holds on to life to movement to response to living she
opens the egg friendlore rest in the nebula dust
brighter than night light for a moment a moon that
does not flicker bruised knees

they enter   the room sucks them in she lays waiting

she pulls the cyan curtains long light earthy they
pinch the tall windows she brings them together the
old room filled with rivers of pastel skies

she holds on to drapes as fluid as constant as present
presence she lies in on ground stratosphere texts in
layers on hazy land she lands

she is the poetic voice in their head she is the poem
they found in fifteen lines

petal.

holding onto

there is only the outer ring ridges on the well
stretch reach out there is only staggering smooth
dome of light knowing being floating forms waves
open overwhelms when depth holds

the sky expansive and porous waver blurred circle
of symmetrical distance the well sits still solid on its
own wild scape isle-land of the land

intimacy we pause we tend we stay in
with within outside inside spheres until five ten
fifteen twenty years broke in glasgow comme un
deluge a cloud burst her well

kind words that tend that mend each time

kreoling love

as poetic as chirps of a cardinal at dusk as tangible as intimacy of
exchange poetry sung in kreol as intimate as flesh island resonance soil
and waves kreoling as intimate as a sister one sleeps with
through childhood and reckons with in adulthood

if february twenty-nine was a revelation a captured moment the
forty eight months dependent of devices was a cycle emblematic
transforming so confirmed a tarot reading there are dates that hold
themselves within a new gravity a nebula a static world an
afterglow from the time and place we live in

she makes space for expansive twilights time zones seasons
climates in a grieved confused closure a route she maintains on a
thread through breath and voice as trail she does not wonder
whether she was pulled or hooked herself to a subcurrent to
continue through the realm of the everyday

she knows it from the smoked earthiness of petrichor

red spirit october seven

and then there are dates in a lifetime that define
presence from metal chants on brixton bars to red
rivers in westminster an unwavering line the same
month a decade ago a deflection a sign crashing into
parliament their frontlines a constance

sister in blood arms

from their mothers waters they call to the discerning
heartbreak red foxlings moon a beginning endless
flaming decades of terror calling back rooks and
crows and seagulls from the square in a court of
justice where dismembered land over disputes abound
two hundred nautical miles and

from the river to the sea

they sit by the road side their legs in meghalayan
clouds on the tube six million chants they summon
collective prayers from pineal crystals from the unrest
from lands ancestral lineage and waters hold five
hundred years of apartheid walls and blood lives for
liberation

seasonal tides

what is it with proximity to the ocean like the front yard of
displacement an anchor a sea bed the pull to the optical end of land the
theory of the grip sound waves the clusters the seagull mwano pikpik
konde the sitting the stillness the ravann the radio waves

motion a summer ritual trust of a three year old screaming to touch the
tip of shore naked a mother loses it soul music two women wrapped in
the sun face the sea the theory of the parallel angle the curve the line
the dot

a father in tracksuit two boys one carries a nonchalant backpack a
twist in his limbs rhythm his round brown waist smothering the water
a five year old girl in a jumpsuit with hood and tiger prints a nine year
old with iconic hair standing against the ocean the theory of gathering
when life permits

when the music is gone they take the chairs with them they move
towards the inland shores we stay the mauve tint on the horizon louder
than the blues

the logic of the arc

they cannot read the skies they dig boxes
deep into   swamps though epiphytic   to find answers to the
icon   to phytology of fenestration the   difference between
positive obsession   and the biocentric sinking folly is in
the continuum of insanity
of the

lines   joined at the molecular   at the transition of matter
water a sign here   the minutiae of stratosphere fossil blood of soil   if
they only looked up   the log the call   perspective the square the
hole the oyster   the astrophysical pearl
way of knowing
opaque for a reason   what
whose reason
why dust are stars that die into cells so
earth and reefs   can swirl into a horizontal stem   that only
we see   before the vials refuse spirit   the translucent
zone   soaked   relief from the shift between
sugar and salt
and flight

that you cannot find with shovel and sieve

un-embalm

the rings of trees remember six storms from constellations
in the last two thousand years

how plants defy gravity with shifts from fluctuation of
spectral dust in the stratosphere

the beagle roamed oceans on extractive terms the weather
clusters beyond unlistened and biology determined outside
the cosmos and ancestral bodies of minds

archaeology now unearthing without ceremony soil and
bones that can never rest that cannot return to the circle of
fallen stars and ocean floors

before flight

how do we write to repair and commune
with the splinters i ask sh.e rises and paces
in the mangroves to point preach rebel is
called upon how to gather in the present and
the possibility voiced in canopy skycries
breezing in and from southern coastal
lands and waters and each other

iel listens

how to walk with and hold one another
we wander across the deck on the sea
to intimately world life history ancestry
weave them in the water struggle under
out feet fresh mud swirling the ocean
beds across sound waves of mountain range
spawning with the fizzle of birds

iel crosses h.er arms

how do we practice self full love with
oneself with others we pause sit in the
wind listen to the screams of dawn
while light before us rotates to the
descent of a moon behind peaks faded
nebulous haze we sit in parallel
thoughts we hear skies take over clouds

return to silver shores

static a delusion watershed h.er stomp un autre
deluge performed as mist blurs ominously skyline
at our door with no step

this time the lagoon spread twice as land luminous
aquamarine a veil over the warnings too late
before the crisis before the closure

under the revelation of colliding storms between
ocean ground and sphere of gaseous sky

she returns sixteen moons since she found herself
from the other sea the far one the roaring one the
morning silence ringing once more

this time she rises with scalding burns in her chest

travelling worlds

we commune from a gathering of particles

shaping ground together/travelling worlds María Lugones. Black study Fred Moten. tongues Gloria Anzaldúa. tenderly/excess salt Christina Sharpe. post-1492/homo narrans/cosmogony Sylvia Wynter. imagine otherwise/performing the future of abolition on the page Saidiya Hartman

Ziwa kuu Yvonne Adhiambo Owuor/Sinthujan Varatharajah. iel the storm. story geography Katherine McKittrick. *mountains on sea* altered *Lava Spasm* Sneha Subramanian Kanta Parentheses Journal. usulu in Emakhuwa my uncle Mozambique. covent garden the rewiring. makook eit Manish Chandi Andaman islands. Simon age 11 1662. *the captive boy and the unwinged biped/unrest two/unrest three* Doek! casuarina burung cenderawasih Syafiqah Jaaffar Belayar: A Voyage of Love and Longing Malay archipelago. ocean breathing Alexis Pauline Gumbs

ungendered Hortense Spillers. Ana and Esperance Soondrun Pavattan Aurélie Marie-Lisette Talate Marie Rose Randamy a continuous rebel line. Kaya carceral violence Lindsey Collen. *kreoling* sisters: (un)intimate relationships, child marriages and women spirits Maria del Pilar Kaladeen Journal for the Study of Indentureship and Its Legacies. Sabrina and Amanda Island Pieces. *lalang twist* first addastories prompted Rajiv Mohabir Mānoa: Pacific Journal of International Writing. *ore oru oorile* tamil twittersphere. Manjula your spirit dwells with us

watersky protectors LAND BACK movements. Zami Audre Lorde. Still I Rise Maya Angelou. ice pick stars Dipa Mahbuba Yasmin. family diaspora and heartbreak

diamonds Rihanna of course. those earthy curtains Oana. *holding onto* altered *there is only sky* Shaimaa Abdelkarim Silver Pinion. red spirit Free Palestine. *before my flight* The Funambulist 43. my first poem Ama Josephine Budge Hsyreita

and to all shifts perceptible in the nebulae

imagine otherwise with

. *Undrowned: Black Feminist Lessons from Marine Mammals* Alexis Pauline Gumbs AK Press 2020

. *Voodoo Hypothesis* Canisia Lubrin Buckrider Books 2017

. *Everyone Knows I Am a Haunting* Shivanee Ramlochan Peepal Tree Press 2017

. *A Map to the Door of No Return: Notes to Belonging* Dionne Brand Vintage Canada 2002

. *The Cowherd's Son* Rajiv Mohabir Tupelo Press 2017

. *The Arrivants: A New World Trilogy* Kamau Brathwaite Oxford University Press 1981

. Venus in Two Acts Saidiya Hartman *Small Axe* no. 26 2008

. *Zom-Fam* Kama La Mackerel Metonymy Press 2020

. *Migritude* Shailja Patel Kaya Press 2010

. Beauty Is a Method Christina Sharpe *e-flux* no. 105 2019

. How to Tame a Wild Tongue? *Borderlands/La Frontera* Gloria Anzaldúa Aunt Lute Books 1987

. *Zami: A New Spelling of My Name A Biomythography* Audre Lorde Persephone Press 1982

www.ingramcontent.com/pod-product-compliance
Lightning Source LLC
Chambersburg PA
CBHW051214090426
42742CB00022B/3455

* 9 7 8 1 4 7 8 0 3 8 5 0 4 *